Guide to Owning an English Bulldog

RE-346

Contents

© by T.F.H. Publications, Inc.

Distributed in the UNITED STATES to the Pet Trade by T.F.H. Publications, Inc., One T.F.H. Plaza, Neptune City, NJ 07753; on the Internet at www.tfh.com; in CANADA Rolf C. Hagen Inc., 3225 Sartelon St. Laurent-Montreal Quebec H4R 1E8; Pet Trade by H & L Pet Supplies Inc., 27 Kingston Crescent, Kitchener, Ontario N2B 2T6; in ENGLAND by T.F.H. Publications, PO Box 15, Waterlooville PO7 6BQ; in AUSTRALIA AND THE SOUTH PACIFIC by T.F.H. (Australia), Pty. Ltd., Box 149, Brookvale 2100 N.S.W., Australia; in NEW ZEALAND by Brooklands Aquarium Ltd. 5 McGiven Drive, New Plymouth, RD1 New Zealand; in SOUTH AFRICA, Rolf C. Hagen S.A. (PTY.) LTD. P.O. Box 201199, Durban North 4016, South Africa; in Japan by T.F.H. Publications, Japan—Jiro Tsuda, 10-12-3 Ohjidai, Sakura, Chiba 285, Japan. Published by T.F.H. Publications, Inc.

MANUFACTURED IN THE
UNITED STATES OF AMERICA
BY T.F.H. PUBLICATIONS, INC.

HISTORY AND ORIGIN OF THE BULLDOG

Paleontologists trace the ancestry of the dog back approximately 55 million years. Climate, purpose, geography, and environmental conditions were factors in the evolution of the dog. Dogs have evolved into several different branches of evolutionary development. The commonly recognized

From these different branches evolved and formed through selective, purposeful breeding the modern-day dog.

Although the exact origin of the modern-day English Bulldog is not known with certainty, it is generally thought that the Bulldog and the Mastiff evolved from the ancient Alaunt—

The tenacious Bulldog has evolved from the ancient Mastiff-like breeds originally used to restrain oxen and hunt wild boar.

paleontological branches were: the gigantic "bear-dogs"; the hyena-type dogs of North America; the wolf-type "dingo" dogs of Southern Asia and Australia; the arctic Pariahs of Asia Minor and Japan; and the Basenji-type dogs of Africa.

regarded as a fierce mastiff-like breed, used to restrain to fierce oxen and to hunt wild boar.

It seems that the word "bulldog" was first used in a 1598 description of a bullbaiting contest. However, it is generally thought that the Bulldog was a

Bred specifically for participation in the now-outlawed sport of bullbaiting, the Bulldog is an important part of the history of England.

well-known, recognized breed in England long before.

"Bandogs," "Bonddoggess," and "Bolddogges" were repeatedly mentioned in English literature beginning around 1200, when the "sport" of bullbaiting and bearbaiting first became popular in England. However, a reference to "British Hounds" that attacked bulls dates back to 395 AD. These dogs were bred and trained to bite and hang on to the noses, ears, and necks of bulls.

The object of the bullbaiting contest was for the Bulldog to seize the bull by the nose and to hang on, without ever relinquishing its hold on the bull. These dog could retain their hold even after their entrails had been torn out, and the dogs often times bled to death from wounds received from the bull. A dog's attack upon the extremities of the bull—but not the nose—called into question the purity of the breed. Litters of Bulldogs as young as six months old were often put through such trials to test the purity of breeding and to rule out the possibility of an improper crossbreeding.

Enthusiasts in the early bull and bearbaiting contests included all classes of people. In 1559, Queen Elizabeth was noted to be a frequent enthusiast and often hosted grand social gatherings centered on the barbaric sport.

At the time, almost every village in England had its own bullring (the town's social center), and vast fortunes were spent on sport-related wagers.

Because of conscientious and responsible breeding, the temperament of the Bulldog has greatly improved. A well-bred Bulldog makes a gentle and devoted companion.

Bullbaiting was also a favorite form of entertainment of the Romans, Egyptians, and Greeks as well. Thus, the dogs were selectively bred for power, courage, and tenacity.

In 1835, bullbaiting and bearbaiting contests were abolished in England by an act of Parliament. After the abolishment, the number of purebred Bulldogs declined greatly, due in large part to the growing popularity of the sport of dog fighting, which replaced bullbaiting as a favorite public amusement in late 19th century England. Breeders began crossbreeding Bulldogs with terrier-type breeds in order to develop a much more agile fighter. Around 1840, the existing Bulldog breed was also widely crossed with a smaller, gentler, "pug-like" dog in order to create a more domesticated housedog.

The Bulldog thus evolved from a sporting dog into a gentler companion, and its existence was preserved by fanciers of the breed in England and France to serve as a household companion and pet.

Ironically, the modern-day English Bulldog, because of its extraordinary calm, kind, and sweet temperament and disposition, is very different from the ferocious and vicious dog from which it evolved.

STANDARD FOR THE BULLDOG

With the advent of dog shows for exhibition purposes in England in 1859, the need arose for a definitive breed "standard of perfection" to be promulgated. The first official breed standard was published in 1865 in England as a guide to serve breeders, exhibitors, and judges of dog shows.

This breed standard has been slightly amended many times by both the National Bulldog Club in England (founded in 1875) and by the Bulldog Club of America (founded in 1890).

Since 1886, when the Bulldog was first admitted to the American Kennel Club registry, the English Bulldog in America has greatly increased in numbers and popularity, both as a companion animal and a show dog.

The Bulldog is truly a lot of dog in a solid small package.

The English Bulldog, or Bulldog (the recognized name given the breed by the American Kennel Club and the Bulldog Club of America), is to be differentiated from other so-called "breeds" that are not recognized by the American Kennel Club. Such breeds include the American Bulldog, and the Pit Bull Terrier. The English Bulldog is bred to have a kind and loving demeanor body, massive short-faced head, wide shoulders and sturdy limbs. The general appearance and attitude should suggest great stability, vigor and strength. The disposition should be equable and kind, resolute and courageous (not vicious or aggressive), and demeanor should be pacific and dignified. These attributes should be countenanced by the expression and behavior.

Giving the appearance of stability and vigor, the ideal Bulldog possesses a thick sturdy body and short smooth coat.

and temperament and certainly is not suitable as a "fighting" dog.

OFFICIAL STANDARD FOR THE BULLDOG

General Appearance—The perfect Bulldog must be of medium size and smooth coat; with heavy, thick-set, low-swung **Size, Proportion, Symmetry**—*Size*—The size for mature dogs is about 50 pounds; for mature bitches about 40 pounds. *Proportion*—The circumference of the skull in front of the ears should measure at least the height of the dog at the shoulders. *Symmetry*—The "points" should

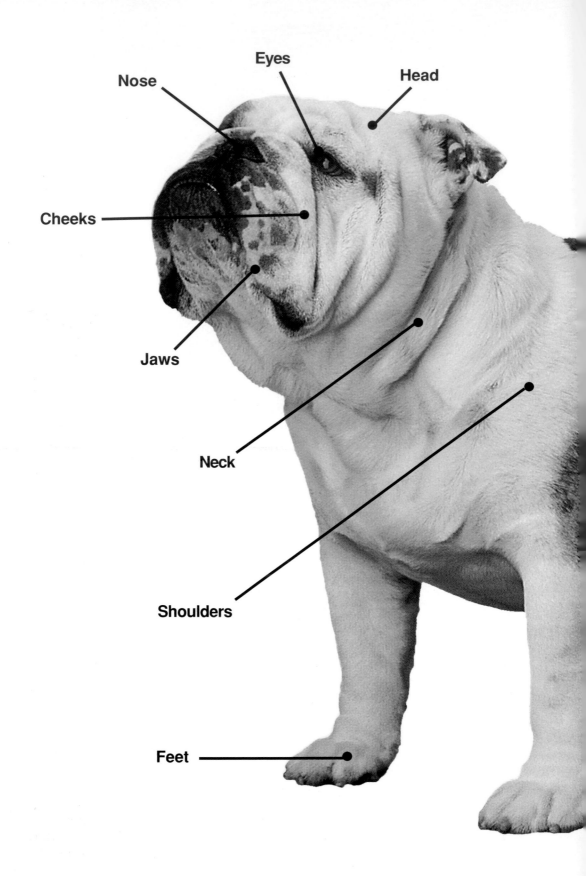

Nose

Eyes

Head

Cheeks

Jaws

Neck

Shoulders

Feet

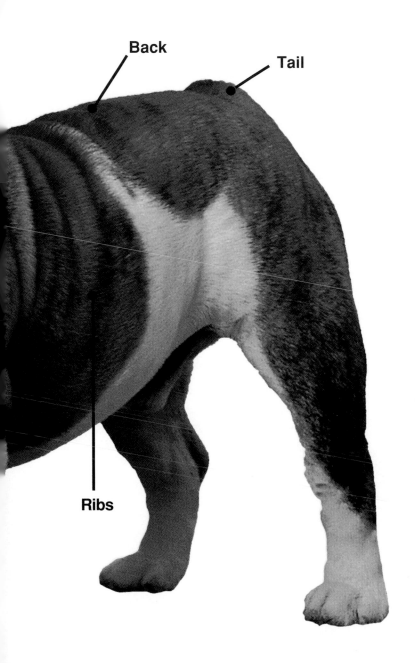

Back

Tail

Ribs

be well distributed and bear good relation one to the other, no feature being in such prominence from either excess or lack of quality that the animal appears deformed or ill-proportioned. *Influence of Sex*—In comparison of specimens of different sex, due allowance should be made in favor of the bitches, which do not bear the characteristics of the breed to the same degree of perfection and grandeur as do the dogs.

Head—*Eyes and Eyelids*—The eyes, seen from the front, should be situated low down in the skull, as far from the ears as possible, and their corners should be in a straight line at right angles with the stop. They should be quite in front of the head, as wide apart as possible, provided their outer corners are within the outline of the cheeks when viewed from the front. They should be quite round

An important characteristic of the breed, the ears of the English Bulldog should fold inward and should never be carried erect.

This Bulldog shows the perfect example of the short muzzle, flat forehead, and rounded cheeks required in the standard.

in form, of moderate size, neither sunken nor bulging, and in color should be very dark. The lids should cover the white of the eyeball, when the dog is looking directly forward, and the lid should show no "haw." *Ears*—The ears should be set high in the head, the front inner edge of each ear joining the outline of the skull at the top back corner of skull, so as to place them as wide apart, and as high, and as far from the eyes as possible. In size, they should be small and thin. The shape termed "rose ear" is the most desirable. The rose ear folds inward at its back lower edge, the upper front edge curving over, outward and backward, showing part of the inside of the burr. (The ears should not be carried erect or prick-eared or buttoned and should never be cropped.) *Skull*—The skull should be very large, and in circumference, in front of the ears, should measure at least the height of the dog at the shoulders. Viewed from the front, it should appear very high from the corner of the lower jaw to the apex of the skull, and also very broad and square. Viewed at the side, the head should appear very high, and very short from the point of the nose to occiput. The forehead should be flat (not rounded or domed), neither too prominent nor overhanging the face. *Cheeks*—The cheeks should be well rounded, protruding sideways and outward beyond the eyes. *Stop*—The temples or frontal bones should be very well defined, broad, square and high, causing a hollow or groove between the eyes. This indentation, or stop, should be both broad and deep and extend up the middle of the forehead, dividing the head vertically, being traceable to the top of the skull. *Face and Muzzle*—The face, measured from the front of the cheekbone to the tip of the nose, should be extremely short, the muzzle being very short, broad, turned upward and very deep from the corner of the eye to the corner of the mouth. *Nose*—The nose should be large, broad and black, its tip set back deeply between the eyes. The distance from bottom of stop, between the eyes, to the tip of nose should be as short as possible and not exceed the length from the tip of nose to the

One of the most recognizable dogs in existence, the Bulldog puppy should be a miniature version of his parents.

edge of underlip. The nostrils should be wide, large and black, with a well-defined line between them. Any nose other than black is objectionable and a brown or liver-colored nose shall **disqualify**. *Lips*—The chops or "flews" should be thick, broad, pendant and very deep, completely overhanging the lower jaw at each side. They join the underlip in front and almost or quite cover the teeth, which should be scarcely noticeable when the mouth is closed. *Bite—Jaws*—The jaws should be massive, very broad, square and "undershot," the lower jaw projecting considerably in front of the upper jaw and turning up. *Teeth*—The teeth should be large and strong, with the canine teeth or tusks wide apart, and the six small teeth in front, between the canines, in an even, level row.

The neck of the Bulldog is short, deep, and very thick and arches down toward his back.

Neck, Topline, Body—*Neck*—The neck should be short, very thick, deep and strong and well arched at the back. *Topline*—There should be a slight fall in the back, close behind the shoulders (its lowest part), whence the spine should rise to the loins (the top of which should be higher than the top of the shoulders), thence curving again more suddenly to the tail, forming an arch (a very distinctive feature of the breed), termed "roach back" or, more correctly, "wheel-back." *Body*—The brisket and body should be very capacious, with full sides, well-rounded ribs and very deep from the shoulders down to its lowest part, where it joins the chest. It should be well let down between the shoulders and forelegs, giving the dog a broad, low, short-legged appearance. *Chest*—The chest should be very broad, deep and full. *Underline*—The body should be well ribbed up behind with the belly tucked up and not rotund. *Back and Loin*—The back should be short and strong, very broad at the shoulders and comparatively narrow at the loins. *Tail*—The tail may be either straight or "screwed" (but never curved or curly), and in any case must be short, hung low, with decided downward carriage, thick root and fine tip. If straight, the tail should be cylindrical and of uniform taper. If "screwed," the bends or kinks should be well defined, and they may be abrupt and even knotty, but no portion of the member should be elevated above the base or root.

Forequarters—*Shoulders*—The shoulders should be muscular, very heavy, widespread and slanting outward, giving stability and great power. *Forelegs*—The

The Bulldog's unique-looking tail is hung low and may either be straight or screwed, but never curved or curly.

forelegs should be short, very stout, straight and muscular, set wide apart, with well developed calves, presenting a bowed outline, but the bones of the legs should not be curved or bandy, nor the feet brought too close together. *Elbows*—The elbows should be low and stand well out and loose from the body. *Feet*—The feet should be moderate in size, compact and firmly set. Toes compact, well split up, with high knuckles and very short stubby nails. The front feet may be straight or slightly out-turned.

Hindquarters—*Legs*—The hind legs should be strong and muscular and longer than the forelegs, so as to elevate the loins above the shoulders. Hocks should be slightly bent and well

let down, so as to give length and strength from the loins to hock. The lower leg should be short, straight and strong, with the stifles turned slightly outward and away from the body. The hocks are thereby made to approach each other, and the hind feet to turn outward. *Feet*—The feet should be moderate in size, compact and firmly set. Toes compact, well split up, with high knuckles and short stubby nails. The hind feet should be pointed well outward.

Coat and Skin—*Coat*—The coat should be straight, short, flat, close, of fine texture, smooth and glossy. (No fringe, feather or curl.) *Skin*—The skin should be soft and loose, especially at the head, neck and shoulders. *Wrinkles and*

There is a color for everyone! The Bulldog's coat can come in a variety of colors, including brindle, shown here.

Dewlap—The head and face should be covered with heavy wrinkles, and at the throat, from jaw to chest, there should be two loose pendulous folds, forming the dewlap.

Color of Coat—The color of coat should be uniform, pure of its kind and brilliant. The various colors found in the breed are to be preferred in the following order: (1) red brindle, (2) all other brindles, (3) solid white, (4) solid red, fawn or fallow, (5) piebald, (6) inferior qualities of all the foregoing. *Note*: A perfect piebald is preferable to a muddy brindle or defective solid color. Solid black is very undesirable, but not so objectionable if occurring to a moderate degree in piebald patches. The brindles to be perfect should have a fine, even and equal distribution of the composite colors. In brindles and solid colors a small white patch on the chest is not considered detrimental. In piebalds the color patches should be well defined, of pure color and symmetrically distributed.

Gait—The style and carriage are peculiar, his gait being a loose-jointed, shuffling, sidewise motion, giving the characteristic "roll." The action must, however, be unrestrained, free and vigorous.

Temperament—The disposition should be equable and kind, resolute and courageous (not vicious or aggressive), and demeanor should be pacific and dignified. These attributes should be countenanced by the expression and behavior.

SCALE OF POINTS

General Properties

Proportion and Symmetry..........5
Attitude 3
Expression 2
Gait 3
Size 3
Coat 2
Color of Coat .... 4—22

Possessing a rolling gait, the Bulldog may walk in a sideways shuffling motion, but his movement should always be free and vigorous.

Head

Skull	5
Cheeks	2
Stop	4
Eyes and Eyelids	3
Ears	5
Wrinkle	5
Nose	6
Chops	2
Jaws	5
Teeth	2—39

Body, Legs, etc.

Neck	3
Dewlap	2
Shoulders	5
Chest	3
Ribs	3
Brisket	2
Belly	2
Back	5
Forelegs and Elbows	4
Hind Legs	3
Feet	3
Tail	4—39
Total	100

DISQUALIFICATION

Brown or liver-colored nose.
Approved July 20, 1976
Reformatted November 28,
1990

INTERPRETING THE BREED STANDARD

The ideal English Bulldog is a medium-sized, compact, short-bodied, short-legged, "low-swung" animal. In order to have the correct appearance, the English Bulldog must be perfectly balanced. The ideal English Bulldog must be of medium size with a thickset body, a massive short-faced head, wide shoulders, and heavy-boned limbs.

The standard requires that the size for mature dogs is "about 50 pounds," and "about 40 pounds" for mature females. Some breeders, fanciers, and exhibitors, however, are of the opinion that the ideal size for the Bulldog is approximately five pounds more than the weight set forth in the standard. Perhaps this is because the modern-day English Bulldog bears little resemblance to the English Bulldog of even 50 years ago. Generally, today's Bulldog is a more compact type with larger

The English Bulldog is commonly referred to as a "head" breed because of his prominent and distinctive features.

head and larger bone mass than its ancestors.

The English Bulldog is commonly referred to as a "head breed." The head of the English Bulldog is one of the most prominent and distinctive features of this breed. The head components and properties (and the properties of proportion, attitude, and expression, totaled together) consist of 49 of the 100 total points of the Bulldog, as set forth in the official standard.

Even as a puppy, the Bulldog should have the dark brown eyes, wide jaw, and short back characteristic of the breed.

Perhaps in no other breed is the head as important as it is in the standard for the Bulldog. The head should be massive in circumference and in length, and the forehead should be flat (not rounded or domed) and not prominent, nor overhanging the face. Generally, females possess smaller heads than males and have less bone mass.

Other important characteristics of the breed are very dark brown, round eyes, a massive, wide, level jaw, and a short back or topline. The topline of this breed is another distinct breed characteristic. Instead of a level or flat topline, the proper English Bulldog's topline dips slightly behind the shoulders (the lowest point of the topline) then rises smoothly and gradually to the loin area. At the loin area, the topline should be higher than as it appears in the shoulder area. At the loin, the topline bends downwards again to the area of the tail, forming an arch. Ideally, the loin area (or top of the rear end) of the dog should be slightly higher than the upper most portion of the shoulder area.

Ears are another important characteristic of the English Bulldog. The ears should be set high on the head and should be small and thin. The "rose ear" is the proper ear for the English Bulldog. The "rose ear" folds backward, showing part of the inside of the burr of the ear. The ears should never be erect, "flyaway," "flopped," or "button-eared."

Another distinct feature of the English Bulldog is the "loose-jointed" nature of the breed. The loose-jointed state of the English Bulldog gives the dog a peculiar style and carriage, constituting a shuffling, sidewise motion, giving it a characteristic rear-end roll. The movement of the dog must be unrestrained, free, and vigorous.

Unlike many other breeds, the official standard of the Bulldog allows for nearly all of the usual colors as being proper. However, the breed standard does list the various preferred colors. The first preference is red brindle; the second, all other brindles; the third, solid white; followed by solid red, fawn or fallow, and piebald (a mostly white coat, coupled with patches of coloration).

As a companion animal, color should have no bearing on the selection of the dog. Interestingly, many new fanciers, when selecting an English Bulldog for the first time, seek a solid white dog as their preferred color. Many breeders and exhibitors, however, seem to have a slight preference for the red brindle color and the dark red (mahogany red) color— combined with white chests, legs, and plenty of white on the face. However, each person has his or her personal preference and particular opinion as to what color or color combination is the most attractive.

Even if your English Bulldog is not destined for the show ring, he'll still make a wonderful companion!

SELECTING AN ENGLISH BULLDOG

Before beginning your search for a puppy, you should ask yourself if the English Bulldog is the proper addition to your family.

Will the new addition receive the necessary time, attention, training, and love from you and your family, even after he is no longer a small, cuddly, cute puppy?

The breed, in general, has many positive features that qualify it as an outstanding choice. The looks, the temperament, and the personality of the English Bulldog are, perhaps, unparalleled. The breed is sweet, lovable, happy, and loyal, and usually more laid back or less nervous and high-strung than most other breeds.

How can you resist that face? Bulldog puppies are adorable, so be sure that the decision add one to your family has been carefully considered.

When properly cared for and socialized, English Bulldogs are sweet, even tempered, and a lot of fun to have around!

However, English Bulldogs should receive daily exercise, but are not as physical as most other breeds, and therefore will require less activity. When properly cared for, this short-haired breed is easy to maintain and usually has very little offensive odor.

Additionally, because of his exceptionally sweet personality and disposition, the English Bulldog generally rates as a poor watchdog—preferring instead to love everyone, including

Your English Bulldog will have a good start in life if his parents are healthy and well adjusted. Try to see the dam and sire of the puppy before making your decision.

unwanted intruders. Some, however, have become excellent watchdogs and guardians.

Bulldogs are perfect homebodies, preferring to spend all their free time next to their owners or sitting on or next to their owners for long periods. They prefer to be housedogs rather than kennel dogs and thrive in a loving home environment where they will receive lots of affection and attention.

However, the breed has several drawbacks. The English Bulldog, even when properly and carefully bred, has more than its fair share of genetic and general health problems. They often snore loudly. Bulldogs, which must always be delivered by Caesarean section, are costly to raise and more costly to purchase than other breeds.

The English Bulldog occasionally suffers from eye problems, primarily entropion, which is an eyelid deformity and often associated with wrinkle-faced breeds. Entropion and other eye diseases can be costly to correct by treatment such as surgery, and dogs with such conditions should never be bred.

Another serious problem in the modern English Bulldog is the propensity to have overly loose and malformed joints. Only a small percentage of English Bulldogs today have hips that are sufficient for Orthopedic

Foundation of America (OFA) certification. The majority has loose and malformed hip sockets and often suffers from varying degrees of hip dysplasia. Joint problems, however, are not limited to the hips, but often also involve shoulders, elbows, and knees as well. In many instances, these joints are either poorly formed or are too loose to allow extremely painful. On many occasions, owners are faced with the decision of having to euthanize a severely dysplastic dog, due to the severity of the pain and suffering involved. An ethical and conscientious breeder will, through a proper breeding program, not breed such animals. Through careful breeding practices, orthopedic problems in

Bulldogs are the perfect homebodies and prefer to spend their time in the company of the people they love.

the dog the necessary support and proper movement. Severe degrees of hip and elbow dysplasia are a problem often seen in the English Bulldog and can, in most cases, lead to the dog's inability to even walk or stand up. The condition is often this breed can be kept to a minimum, as can most other genetic health problems.

English Bulldogs sometimes also suffer from allergies and the resultant skin problems that can be caused by a number of allergens, including fleas, pollen,

The English Bulldog is extremely sensitive to heat and should never be subjected to high temperatures. Always have shelter and water for your Bulldog when he is outside.

chemicals, grass, and specific items contained in dog food, such as soy, wheat, or corn.

Another drawback to the breed is that the average life span of an English Bulldog is approximately eight years, relatively short in the canine world.

It is critical to remember that the English Bulldog is an extremely heat-sensitive breed and will ordinarily suffer breathing distress, excessive panting and rasping, and heat stroke (often resulting in death) if subjected to high heat. Special care and precaution should be taken not to subject the English Bulldog to temperatures above 80 degrees Fahrenheit.

For this reason, English Bulldogs should always be kept either in air conditioning or cool shade whenever the temperature becomes dangerous to the dog.

Home sweet home! Bulldogs should always have a cool place to retire to when outside for his health and well-being.

Literally thousands of English Bulldogs have met a tragic death due to heat stroke, whether confined in a hot car, yard, or even inside a home or apartment that suffered the failure or interruption of its air conditioning system.

When you have decided to commit yourself to purchasing an English Bulldog puppy, you should use extra care and caution in making such an important decision.

In this breed, more so than any others, you would be well advised to see and carefully observe both parents of the puppy, as well as all other dogs on the breeder's premises. Carefully evaluate their overall condition. Look for eye problems, abnormalities, and eye irritations. Evaluate the overall appearance of each adult animal. Does he look healthy? Look for skin problems. Look for breathing problems (excessive, loud panting and rasping even in cool temperatures). Look for possible orthopedic problems. Do the adult dogs move vigorously and freely without limping? Do the adults appear to have good, outgoing temperaments and dispositions, or are they overly aggressive, shy, or nervous?

It is important to know the answers to all of these questions because chances are that at one year of age, your little puppy will very closely resemble (although maybe not in coloration and markings) the adults, for better or worse.

English Bulldogs can sometimes suffer from allergies to pollen or grass. Be sure to watch your Bulldog for any reaction when he is outdoors.

It is certainly preferable to spend a bit more effort, time, and money up front in carefully selecting your puppy through a thoughtful and careful process than to rush out and just buy the first puppy you come across. Remember that evaluating both the puppy's parents is very important.

Additionally, buying a puppy from the newspaper classified ads

While there is certainly no guarantee, the preferred source from which to purchase a puppy or young dog is a successful, ethical, and experienced breeder who breeds and shows quality English Bulldogs. Of course, not every "show person" breeds or exhibits dogs of quality. Certainly not every person who shows dogs is ethical. This is where it pays to do your homework—ask other

The care and attention that a reputable breeder gives a Bulldog puppy will be evident in his good temperament and overall healthy appearance.

doesn't always bring good results. Is the breeder knowledgeable, successful, experienced, and ethical? On the other hand, is the breeder a "backyard breeder" who just puts two dogs of average quality together and hopes for the best, without any regard to the genetic background of the sire or the dam?

English Bulldog owners or other breeders for information, suggestions, and help in locating a reputable breeder of quality English Bulldogs. The Bulldog Club of America's breeder referral "contact person" in your area can be located by contacting the Bulldog Club of America. The club can be contacted through the

Curiosity may have got the cat in trouble, but it never hurt a Bulldog! The Bulldog you choose should be bright eyed, alert, and interested in the world around him.

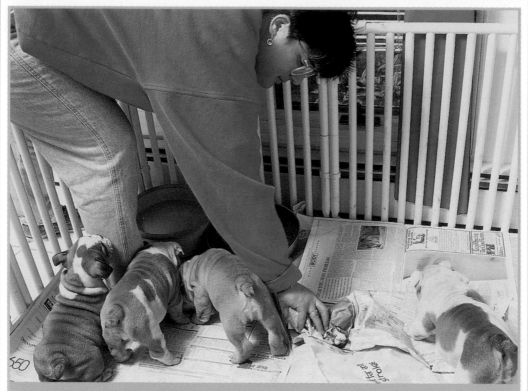

Make sure the breeder that you are dealing with runs a quality facility and that all the puppies are clean, healthy-looking, and well taken care of.

Play with the puppy you are considering away from his littermates. This will give you a better idea of his personality and allow him to get used to you and your family.

Internet, and maintains a World Wide Web page. Also, outstanding adult pets can usually be obtained through the various Bulldog rescue networks, which are set up in all areas of the United States. Both the Bulldog Club of America and its local member club in your area will put you in contact with the network, which rescues English Bulldogs from animal shelters or from people who are no longer able or willing to care for these animals. There are many advantages to obtaining an adult dog rather than a young puppy, and this option should be carefully considered.

Another important suggestion is to be patient in the event the recommended breeder does not have a litter or a puppy available at the time you call.

When selecting the puppy out of a litter, do not automatically choose the most heavily wrinkled pup in the litter. Excessive or exaggerated wrinkles are not a desired trait in the English Bulldog. Such a dog may very well turn out to be "overdone" in the face, and such dogs are often much more prone to eye, skin, and even breathing problems.

Also, remember that the largest puppy is not automatically the best. With English Bulldogs, bigger is not better. The breed is a compact, medium-sized, low-swung dog. Oversized or leggy dogs are often looked upon with disfavor in the show ring, and are not desired for breeding purposes.

Although most prospective new owners cannot refuse the allure of an extremely cute eight-week-old English Bulldog puppy, most of the health and genetic problems that the dog may later develop are rarely visible at this age. For this reason, many people prefer to obtain an older puppy or young adult. By the time the puppy is approximately six months of age, both the owner and the owner's veterinarian can obtain a much clearer indication of whether any serious health problems are present or will arise in the future. Rarely can this be said about an eight-week-old puppy.

The breeder will have started feeding your puppy a high-quality dog food formulated for growth. Continue this diet until your puppy matures.

To ensure against genetic diseases and to produce the best puppies possible, responsible breeders will screen all Bulldogs before breeding them.

Should you decide to obtain a young puppy, take ample time to study and evaluate the entire litter. Select only a puppy that radiates good health and spirit. Select a puppy whose coat shines, who moves eagerly, who is bright-eyed and lively, but not hyperactive.

Additionally, you should question the breeder regarding

Most importantly, always get a written bill of sale from the breeder that contains a provision allowing you to return the puppy for a full refund, for any reason, within 72 hours of purchase. This will enable you to bring the puppy to your veterinarian in order to have it examined. In the event that the veterinarian discovers any serious health problem, you

Puppies are very vulnerable and will need to be vaccinated against certain diseases. It is important to get your new Bulldog to the veterinarian within 72 hours of acquiring him.

health problems present in any of the adults and potentially in the puppies. Always look for the socially outgoing and friendly puppy. Avoid any puppy that is shy or timid.

Whenever possible, get an experienced, reputable breeder to examine the litter with you and to assist in making your selection from the litter.

will usually be allowed the opportunity to return the puppy to the seller for a full refund. Remember, however, no matter how conscientious, ethical, and careful a breeder is, health and genetic defects will occasionally surface that are completely beyond the control of the breeder. Also, the vast majority of health problems and genetic defects do not surface until such time as the puppy becomes an adult, and the breeder may not even be aware of the genetic or health problem.

BRINGING BABY HOME

As soon as you receive your English Bulldog puppy or dog, you should also receive from the seller a record of the dog's immunizations and wormings and documentation that says the puppy has been examined by a veterinarian, along with the name and telephone number of the vet. When you arrive home with your puppy or young dog, keep in mind that the puppy is similar to a human baby and needs lots of

Socialization with littermates when young will ensure that your Bulldog will get along with other dogs later in life.

Early socialization with all kinds of people, especially children, is the key to an even-tempered Bulldog puppy.

Give your new Bulldog plenty of love and affection when he first arrives at his new home. The bond you create with him will last a lifetime.

love, affection, and cuddling, as well as plenty of rest and sleep. High-quality, nourishing dog food is also essential, and fresh water should be available at all times.

Joining a new household is an extremely traumatic time for the puppy. For the first two weeks, attempt to follow the breeder's feeding routine as closely as possible. Feed him the same brand of dog food and the same supplements, if any, and stay on the same schedule as the breeder. In the event that you wish to switch to a different brand of dog food, switch the dog food gradually.

English Bulldogs are creatures of habit and should be fed with the same bowl in the same place at each meal. The English Bulldog puppy or dog should also be given his own area for play and sleep. Those first two weeks are extremely important for purposes of bonding and formation of the dog's temperament and personality. Make certain that the puppy is given an abundance of affection and cuddling.

CARING FOR YOUR ENGLISH BULLDOG

The English Bulldog is a unique and special breed. English Bulldogs give their owners an abundance of love, attention, and affection. In return, the owner of an English Bulldog should, at the very least, take extremely good care of his Bulldog. The first step in caring for English Bulldogs should be the selection of a competent and skilled veterinarian who knows and likes the breed. The veterinarian should give your newly acquired Bulldog a thorough examination and make certain that the dog is on a suitable vaccination, worm-prevention, and flea-prevention regimen.

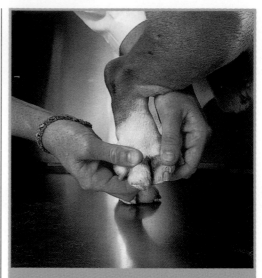

Inspect your Bulldog's feet regularly for cracked pads and keep his toenails short to prevent injuries.

NAILS

English Bulldogs need their nails cut on a regular basis, approximately every three to four weeks. Their nails should be kept as short as possible by using either an electric grinder or nail clippers. Excessively long nails often lead to foot and orthopedic problems.

WRINKLES

The attendant wrinkles of English Bulldogs present some additional problems specific to this breed. The Bulldog's nose and facial wrinkles should be cleaned on a daily basis. Zinc oxide diaper ointment can be used to lessen the bacterial and yeast accumulations in the wrinkles. Such ointments are also effective in treating, preventing, or lessening the "tear stains" often seen in English Bulldogs.

CRATES AND BEDDING

If your aim is to show your English Bulldog puppy and travel

If you accustom your English Bulldog to grooming procedures like nail trimming as a puppy, he will come to accept them as part of his routine care.

An electric nail grinder can be used to keep your English Bulldog's nails trim.

Your Bulldog's nose and facial wrinkles should cleaned on a daily basis to lessen the bacterial and yeast accumulation that could cause infection.

with him, then you should get him used to sleeping in a crate at an early age. As he gets older, the puppy will find solace, comfort, and security while sleeping in the crate. Crates are extremely beneficial for those who plan to travel overnight with their dogs. The crate provides a safe haven, but it should never become a prison for the animal. Dogs should not be confined to their crates for excessive periods. However, most willingly prefer to go into their crates to sleep at night.

The use of crates can also be beneficial for housebreaking purposes, as further mentioned in this book. Cotton rugs or

Bulldogs are housedogs and are happiest when allowed free access to your home.

blankets, which can be washed with ease, make good, soft bedding material for your dog. The artificial sheepskin rugs available from pet stores and many dog-product catalogs also make excellent bedding material. Many Bulldogs get great enjoyment from lying or sleeping on the new, square plastic-frame dog beds made out of nylon mesh material, which are suspended off the floor like a hammock.

GET A BULLDOG VETERINARIAN

It is imperative that any owner of an English Bulldog puppy or adult finds and keeps a competent and skilled veterinarian who knows and likes English Bulldogs. The vast majority of veterinarians do not possess these traits and qualities. Usually, fellow breeders in your area or fellow members of your Bulldog club are more than willing to provide you with the names of qualified English Bulldog veterinarians. This information can also be obtained by contacting the Bulldog Club of America or its local member club in your area. The Bulldog Club of America also provides its

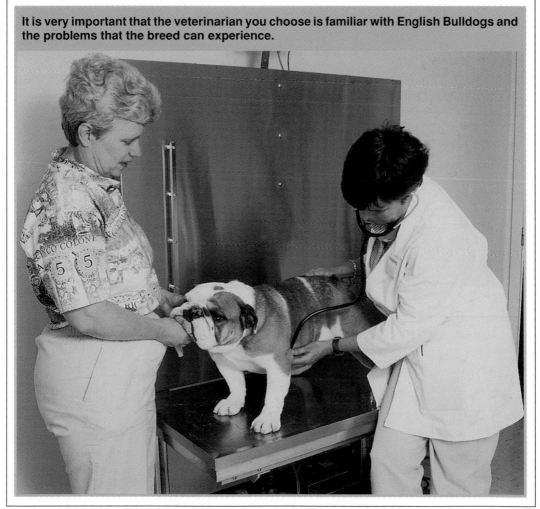

It is very important that the veterinarian you choose is familiar with English Bulldogs and the problems that the breed can experience.

members with the excellent breed publication, *The Bulldogger*, distributed without charge and published on a quarterly basis. *The Bulldogger* provides plenty of detailed, helpful information on the health and care of the breed, and often contains articles written by noted Bulldog veterinarians, as well as many high-quality color photographs of various show dogs being exhibited around the country. Even for those who are not interested in showing dogs,

overly excited Bulldog is also prone to overheat. Therefore, it is imperative to keep your English Bulldog both calm and cool, especially in the summertime. Once the dog becomes overheated, the risk of death or brain damage is quite substantial. If the dog does become overheated, immediate action should be taken to cool him down using cold air or cold water, and in all emergency cases, your veterinarian should be contacted immediately.

This guy is "flat-out" exhausted! Bulldogs have a low tolerance for exercise and can get easily overheated. Make sure you keep your Bulldog calm and cool at all times and see that he gets plenty of rest.

this publication is highly recommended and will prove itself both informative and helpful to any owner of an English Bulldog.

HEAT AND OVEREXCITEMENT

Like all short-nosed breeds, English Bulldogs do not tolerate heat. During the summer months they must be kept cool and in an air conditioned environment. An

CHERRY EYES

The gland that is normally located under the lower eyelid at the inside corner of the eye will often "pop out" in young puppies. Although this is an unsightly nuisance, the appearance of a cherry eye does not require emergency treatment. However, the puppy or dog should be presented to a qualified English

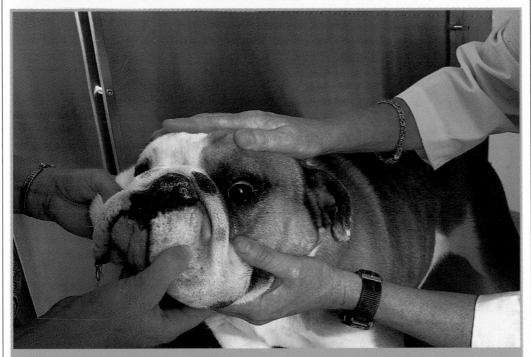

Your English Bulldog's eyes should always be dark, clear, and free from any redness or irritation.

Bulldog veterinarian so that the swollen gland can be surgically tacked. It is no longer an acceptable practice for the veterinarian to cut out or remove the swollen gland because to do so greatly increases the chances that the dog will develop a dangerous "dry-eye," caused by a reduction in tear production, later in life.

TAIL

Unfortunately, many English Bulldogs have exceptionally tight set or short screw-type tails. Efforts need to be made in order to keep folds of skin around the base of the tail clean and dry. Wipe and clean the inside of the tail frequently. Make certain that the area is thoroughly dried and apply a drying powder or an ointment in order to deter the accumulation of yeast and bacteria in the area.

ICE

It is a good idea to provide your English Bulldog puppy with pieces of ice to eat at an early age. This is a special treat because most English Bulldogs love ice. Ice provides an enjoyable chewing opportunity for the dog and is an excellent method of cooling down a dog that is too hot.

CHEWING

Nylabone® and Gumabone® products are excellent and safe and will provide your dog with many hours of chewing enjoyment. It should be noted that all English Bulldogs like and need to chew, especially while

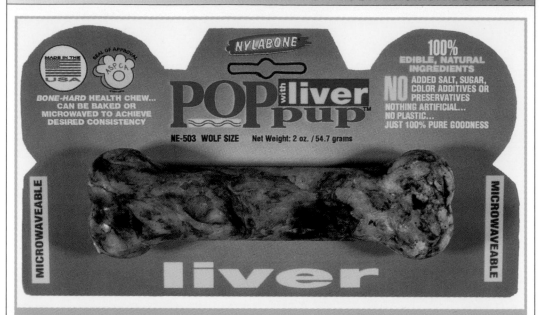

The POPpup™ is a healthy treat for your Bulldog. Its bone-hard consistency helps control plaque and when microwaved, it becomes a rich cracker that your English Bulldog will love.

their teeth and jaws are developing. Such chewing induces growth of permanent teeth, assists in the removal of puppy teeth at the suitable time, and

Not only will your English Bulldog have fun playing tug-of-war with Nylafloss™ he will be flossing his teeth while he pulls.

assists in the development of the jaw. Chewing also helps in keeping teeth clean as well as relieving stress and tension. Puppies and young dogs will often chew everything in sight if not provided with something proper to chew. An English Bulldog should not be permitted to chew on anything that can break or be ingested. Sharp pieces of any substance, such as bone, bark, twigs, rocks, etc., may pierce the intestinal wall and result in death.

Latex dog toys, which cannot be chewed into pieces or ingested, make ideal toys and chew items. Under no circumstances should rawhide bones or any rawhide toys be provided! Rawhide is extremely dangerous and often causes English Bulldogs to choke, since it swells when wet. Also, pieces of rawhide are not easily digestible and can block intestines, which can be fatal. Never provide your puppy or dog with old shoes to play with, either. Very few dogs are able to differentiate between old shoes and new shoes.

BATHING AND THE DANGER OF WATER

Ordinarily, an English Bulldog requires bathing once or twice a month. Overbathing can deplete essential oils from the dog's skin, resulting in skin problems. Commercially prepared flea shampoos are often excessively harsh and serve very little purpose because you should have your English Bulldog on a once-a-month, flea-preventive gel anyway. Mild human or baby shampoos are recommended for bathing. It is extremely important

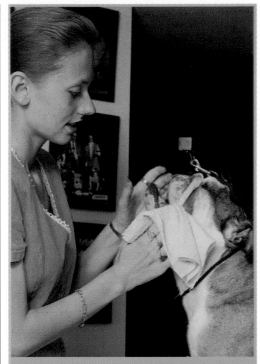

A thorough oral exam should be a part of your English Bulldog's annual veterinary check up.

English Bulldogs require some vegetable matter in their diet and the CarrotBone™ by Nylabone® provides plaque control, satisfies the need to chew, and is nutritious.

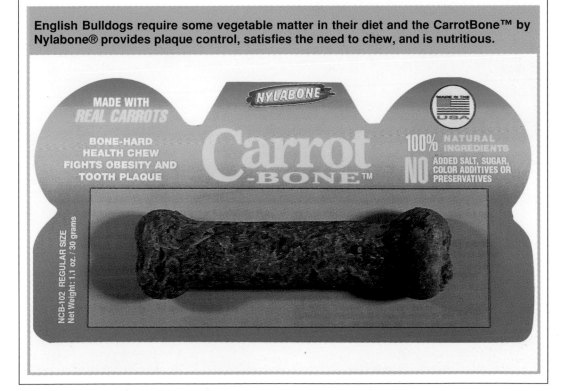

Bulldogs and water are a dangerous combination—this is one breed that should stay out of the pool! Always carefully supervise your English Bulldog around water to keep him safe.

to remember that Bulldogs and water are a dangerous combination. If a Bulldog falls into a swimming pool or lake, the chances are that he will quickly drown. Likewise, an English Bulldog can easily drown while in a bathtub. Never squirt water anywhere near an English Bulldog's nose or mouth. Take special precautions to make sure that water does not drip or drain into the nose or mouth from the forehead. A Bulldog's face should only be cleaned with a wet wash towel. A small amount of shampoo on the facial area is sometimes needed, but should be carefully rinsed out.

Pay particular attention to thoroughly cleaning the area under the wrinkle that appears over the nose of the dog, as well as on the forehead and inside the

You should clean your Bulldog's face and skin daily with a wet wash towel.

Your English Bulldog's ears should be kept clean and free of waxy build up.

reactions from fleas. Flea infestation should be avoided. Flea collars should be not be used as they are usually ineffective and dangerous to English Bulldogs. In fact, in order to prevent your English Bulldog from accidentally choking or hanging himself, no collar should ever be left on an English Bulldog, under any circumstances. A collar should only be used in conjunction with a leash and only while the dog is being walked or leash-handled.

Once-a-month flea treatments (gels that are absorbed along the spine of the dog) are particularly effective as a flea preventative. Always consult your veterinarian and follow the label directions. Note that these preparations are

ears. Use towels to dry the dog after all of the shampoo has been carefully and properly rinsed off. Carefully use cotton swabs to remove any wax build up inside the ear canal. Periodically clean out any wax and debris in the ear canal with liquid ear cleaning solutions.

It is a good idea to clean the Bulldog's wrinkles, ears, and under the folds of skin around the base of the tail between baths, at least once a week. Otherwise, skin and ear infections are a certain result. It is recommended that you put a soothing baby ointment, preferably containing zinc oxide, inside a deep nose wrinkle.

FLEA CONTROL

English Bulldogs are more prone than most dogs to allergic

Good oral hygiene is an important part of your English Bulldog's overall health.

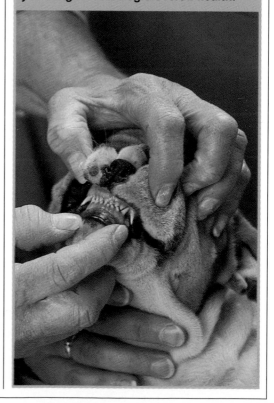

Your Bulldog can pick up parasites like fleas and ticks while in the great outdoors. Be sure to check his coat thoroughly after playing outside.

Rub-a-dub-dub! English Bulldogs will only need an occasional bath and when in the tub, care should be taken not to get water in his face, nose, or eyes.

Your English Bulldog is susceptible to all kinds of parasites when outside. Make sure he has all his vaccinations before taking him out to play.

Your Bulldog must become accustomed to wearing his collar and leash when outside, not only for his safety, but for the safety of others as well.

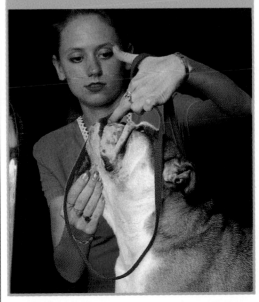

not always suitable for young puppies.

COLLARS

Because of their constricted airways, English Bulldogs' collars should never be left on, except when being walked on a leash. Collars tend to catch on chairs, fences, trees, and other objects—usually resulting in a death by choking or strangulation. Likewise, it is also extremely dangerous to tie or chain a Bulldog up for even a brief moment.

When using a collar and leash during training and daily walks, be careful not to accidentally choke your dog. The chain-type "choke" collars should be avoided.

FEEDING YOUR ENGLISH BULLDOG

Due to his short-faced mouth, an English Bulldog should be provided with a feeding pan that has a flat bottom and is large in circumference. The new stainless steel feeding bowls with the rubber-rimmed, non-skid bases are ideal. The same type of bowl is good for providing fresh water, which should always be available throughout the course of the day and night.

Another option for providing constant fresh water is an automatic nozzle device that can be purchased at most pet stores. The nozzle attaches to a faucet and releases water only upon pressure on the nozzle by the dog's tongue.

DOG FOOD

Until he is approximately four months of age, an English Bulldog puppy should be fed four times a day. Most breeders use a high-quality, dry dog food. A puppy formula is used until the dog is approximately one year of age. English Bulldogs do particularly

Because of his short face and small mouth, your English Bulldog should be provided with a large flat feeding pan for easy access to his meals.

well on high-quality lamb and rice formulas. Care should be taken to make certain that the dog food that you use does not contain any soy or soybean ingredients. Also, dog food brands that contain the chemical preservative ethoxoquin should be avoided, as many believe that this chemical is responsible for causing a number of serious health problems in dogs.

There are several feeding methods and options available. Some breeders feed their English Bulldog puppies and dogs on a set schedule, while others have food available for consumption at all times. In most cases, a thriving, growing puppy that is provided with ample exercise should eat as much as he wants. If the puppy or dog becomes overweight, the

It is fine to give your Bulldog the occasional treat as long as it is nutritious and does not upset his regular meals.

If you put your Bulldog on a regular feeding schedule, he will always know when it's time for supper.

amount of food may need to be regulated. However, a growing puppy should never be put on a severely restrictive diet unless done so by a veterinarian that is knowledgeable about English Bulldogs. Once the puppy reaches six months of age, the number of feedings he receives can be reduced to two per day. As your English Bulldog reaches an advanced age, he may become less active and obese. In this instance, it may be necessary to restrict the amount of food given to the dog.

It is also a good idea to give puppies and dogs a vitamin and mineral supplement, as well as one Vitamin C tablet (100-500 units) per day. Care should be taken not to overdose or

Provide your Bulldog puppy with a varied and nutritious diet formulated for his stage of life.

Your Bulldog will have tons of fun playing with the Nylabone® Frisbee™ and keeping his teeth and gums healthy.

Also, when choosing a brand of dry dog food, you should pay particular attention to the first few (or predominant) ingredients listed on the label of the bag. Ingredients such as lamb, chicken, or brown rice are more preferable than ingredients such as chicken meal, chicken byproducts, ground corn, or lamb meal. Diets with a large amount of corn, corn meal, ground corn, corn hulls, wheat, or peanut hulls will usually prove to be of inferior nutritional value. Dry dog food diets with predominant ingredients such as pure chicken, pure turkey, pure lamb, etc., are usually of much higher quality and of greater benefit to your pet.

oversupplement the dog since harm may result. Particular attention should be paid to guard against oversupplementing Vitamins D and A, which, when provided in excess, can cause problems.

Most breeders avoid using canned dog foods, believing them to be nutritionally inferior to high-quality, dry dog foods. Others cite an increase in gum disease and tooth decay as a result of solely using a canned dog food diet. Others dislike the quick spoilage of canned dog foods. However, many people mix a small amount of canned food with the dry food.

When providing your dog with feeding supplementations such as table scraps, the table scraps should be added to and thoroughly mixed with the dog's dry food. A detrimental pattern can result from feeding your dog directly from your table—the dog may gradually refuse to eat his dry dog food and become a finicky eater.

A healthy and complete diet will be evident in your English Bulldog's shiny coat and overall good condition.

Sometimes even off-brand or generic and cheaper, lesser-known lamb and rice dry dog foods are superior to the more expensive and well-known dog foods—including even those expensive formulas sold primarily through veterinarians. Interestingly, several of the

Until the puppy reaches one year of age, he should be fed a dry puppy formula dog food, preferably lamb and rice. Young puppies will have difficulty eating the dry food, and will need it moistened with water.

Although some believe that it is unnecessary to add supplements

Your breeder will have started your Bulldog puppy on the road to good nutrition, so stick with this original diet when you first bring him home.

brands sold only by the veterinarians are both overpriced and inferior, as a quick glance to the label of ingredients will reveal.

The degree of quality among dry dog foods can be discerned by using your sense of smell. Does it smell bland or odorless? Does it smell like fresh lamb or poultry? The highly processed dry food will usually smell bland.

to a good-quality, dry dog food, many believe that since all dry and canned dog foods are highly processed—no matter how good their ingredients—supplementation with fresh foods is beneficial. Small amounts of cottage cheese, meat, chicken, yogurt, scrambled eggs, granola, cheese, and canola oil are good choices. So, too, are cooked beef

Pick a good-quality dog food that is made for your Bulldog's age and health requirements.

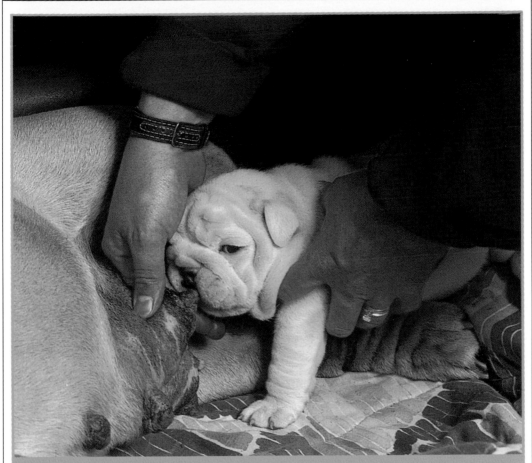

As a puppy, your English Bulldog will get all his nutrients from his mother. Once weaned, however, you will have to provide him with the care and nutrition he needs to stay healthy.

and chicken entrails and livers. It is okay to mix table scraps that do not contain bones or bone matter directly into your dog's food. English Bulldogs should never be allowed to chew on meat bones of any kind, unless supervised carefully. The throats of English Bulldogs are constricted, and they are prone to choking on bones and pieces of bones and other matter. Such choking often leads to death. Also, bone pieces are sharp and can easily pierce the dog's stomach or intestines. If your dog ever appears to be choking or appears to have a blocked airway, immediately reach your hand into the throat and pull out any foreign material or any accumulation of saliva or foam. Lemon juice can be squirted into the throat to help clear it out and to reduce any saliva or foam accumulation.

SPECIAL TREATS

Special treats should be limited to high-quality dog biscuits, which are beneficial to the dog's teeth. A dog should never be provided with any amount of chocolate or onions, as both are toxic to dogs.

HOUSEBREAKING AND TRAINING YOUR ENGLISH BULLDOG

Unlike other breeds, the English Bulldog does not respond well to negative training (i.e., being yelled at, scolded, or hit). Instead, the English Bulldog—both for housebreaking and training purposes—responds much more favorably to positive reinforcement training. When the puppy wakes up each morning, immediately take him outside to the area where you want him to relieve himself. Once he is done, offer him positive praise, reinforcement, and physical affection. Act like you are excited that the puppy has "done it in the right spot." Then, throughout the day, repeat the procedure with the puppy every two hours. Remember that a young puppy is physically unable to keep from urinating or relieving himself any longer. In this regard, your patience is necessary.

If you take your Bulldog puppy to the same place to eliminate every time, he will always know what is expected of him.

Confine your English Bulldog to a safe area of the house when you cannot supervise him.

For those of us who are unable to be with the young puppy throughout the course of the entire day and to housebreak him through the "two-hour method," other methods are available. The puppy can be confined to a small area with his food, water, bedding materials, play toys, etc., on one end, and newspapers should be placed in a large area at the

Bulldogs can be trained to do almost anything! The tenacity, strength, and power that the breed represents makes him a favorite mascot of team sports around the country.

Every dog can benefit from basic obedience training. Dudley, owned by Frieda McCullough, awaits his next command.

opposite end of the confined space. Every day or so, use fewer and fewer newspapers, until the puppy is able to use a single, small area of newspaper. Upon returning home from work, picking up and throwing away the soiled newspaper will be made a lot easier. Remember that accidents will happen, and that full housebreaking often takes several months to accomplish.

Once the puppy reaches approximately six months of age, he progressively gains more and more control over relieving himself as his bladder grows in size and strength and his muscles develop.

OBEDIENCE TRAINING

In order for both the dog and the dog owner to thrive in any dog-person relationship, it is essential that the puppy or dog be given the privilege of being trained. A well-mannered, well-adjusted English Bulldog is an ideal companion.

At the very least, your English Bulldog should be trained to

Walking on a leash is one of the most important things you can teach your Bulldog. Once mastered, he can move on to obedience commands.

instantly come to you when called and to sit when commanded. He should also be trained to have good manners and to exhibit politeness in all circumstances. Politeness and mannerly behavior should be exhibited to people, other dogs, and even to cats.

Obedience Training Class

In the event you do not wish to use a professional dog trainer to train your English Bulldog, another option is to train him by taking in a local obedience training class. Dog obedience classes and clubs are found in nearly every community. The typical obedience class is low cost, non-profit, meets one night a week, and lasts approximately eight weeks. Many owners feel that there is a distinct advantage to training their dogs themselves versus having a professional trainer teach their dog for them. Remember, the goal is to have the dog obey you and to exhibit good manners and politeness in your presence, not to obey only the professional trainer.

The telephone numbers of hundreds of local dog training clubs sanctioned by the AKC can be obtained by contacting the American Kennel Club. They will provide you with the name and

Your English Bulldog will learn basic obedience commands, like down, in a training class.

telephone number of the local club in your area. This information can also be obtained by contacting the AKC on Internet. It maintains a large presence on the World Wide Web, as does the Bulldog Club of America.

Contrary to popular belief, the English Bulldog (provided positive training methods are used) is an easily trained dog. In fact, the author had an English Bulldog of a particularly lazy nature that earned an AKC obedience title with very little effort and training. Hundreds of English Bulldogs have earned AKC obedience titles and certificates, and have excelled in obedience competition against other breeds.

Remember that Bulldogs do not respond favorably to negative training and scolding (in large part due to their extremely sensitive nature). All training should be positive, fun, and filled with praise and encouragement.

The typical eight-week training class usually lasts one hour, one night per week, and may very well prove to be the most enjoyable and rewarding experience for both you and your English Bulldog.

SHOWING YOUR ENGLISH BULLDOG

Although any English Bulldog with a full American Kennel Club registration can enter and compete in a dog show, a true "show-quality" English Bulldog is an extremely rare commodity. Most often, numerous litters of English Bulldog puppies must be bred until a truly outstanding specimen, closely approximating the standard by which the breed is judged in the show ring, is born. A true "show-quality" English Bulldog should be able to obtain his championship on his own merits in a relatively short period. An English Bulldog with a championship is more desired for breeding purposes, both as a stud dog and as a dam.

As a novice exhibitor, you will have to compete against both experienced breeders and professional handlers, both of whom will have numerous and various advantages over you in the ring. Use this as an opportunity to absorb and learn much from the more experienced fellow exhibitors.

At a dog show, the key element is the conformation of the individual dog. A judge's duty is to carefully examine the dogs in

The versatile English Bulldog can perform in many activities and events. This Bulldog participates in a tracking test.

each class and place them according to how well they compare to the breed standard, as well as to the other entrants. In order to compete for championship points, the dog must be at least six months of age on the day of the show. Dogs that are spayed or neutered are ineligible, as are dogs with disqualifying faults as outlined in their particular breed standard.

Most dogs entered in dog shows are competing for points towards their championship. Most do not achieve championship status. To become an AKC champion, a dog must earn 15 points. These points are based on the number of dogs in actual competition. The more dogs that compete, the more points awarded. The number of

A well-trained English Bulldog is a joy to own and a valuable member of any household.

Successful showing requires dedication and preparation, but should be an enjoyable experience for dog and handler alike.

In conformation, your English Bulldog will be judged on how closely he conforms to the breed standard.

dogs required for points varies with the breed's sex and geographical location of the show in accordance with a schedule set up annually by the American Kennel Club.

In addition to conformation shows, English Bulldogs are also eligible to compete in AKC obedience competitions and AKC performance events, such as agility. If your only objective in obtaining an English Bulldog is to get a top-quality show dog, then you would be well served to purchase a puppy that is at least five or six months of age from a highly reputable breeder with good references. It is usually easier and cheaper to acquire a show-quality male than a female. For the novice owner, the selection of the show dog should be made not by the novice owner, but rather by an experienced exhibitor—but buyer beware. When it comes to Bulldog exhibitors, there are honest and successful breeders. However, there are also many dishonest and successful breeders. Here, again, it pays to do your homework. Also, keep in mind that a high number of champions in a puppy's pedigree is no guarantee and no indication that the puppy will be of high conformation quality or high quality for breeding purposes. Many English Bulldogs of poor and mediocre quality have obtained AKC confirmation championships. Not every AKC champion is a deserving, outstanding, representative of the breed.

Competing in a conformation or obedience show is great fun for you and your dog. To find an upcoming show in your area, contact the American Kennel Club.

There are many fine books and tapes to help you learn about grooming and handling a dog in the show ring. Hands-on instruction classes are also beneficial; all-breed kennel clubs in your area routinely offers such handling classes. Additionally, all-breed fun matches and practice matches, hosted by local kennel clubs, can be beneficial and entertaining. By joining your local Bulldog Club of America member club, you will have the benefit of meeting and becoming friends with breeders and exhibitors in your area, who will usually be more than eager to give you friendship, advice, assistance, and encouragement.

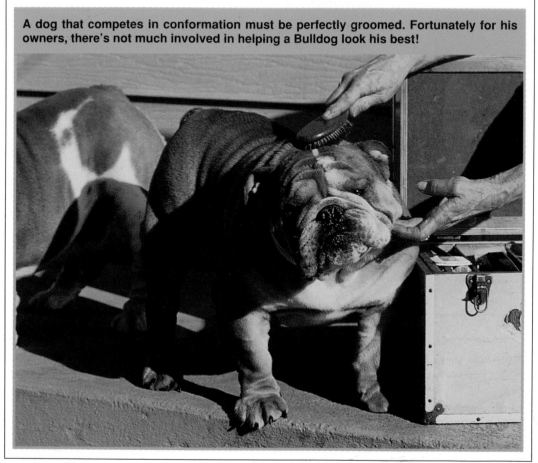

A dog that competes in conformation must be perfectly groomed. Fortunately for his owners, there's not much involved in helping a Bulldog look his best!

SUGGESTED READING

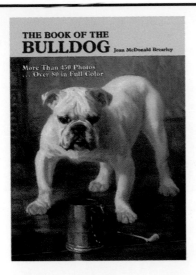

H-1071
Book of the Bulldog
Joan McDonald Breaerly
300 pages, over 300 full-color photos

JG-139
A New Owner's Guide
to Bulldogs
Hank and Carol Williams
160 pages, over 150 full-color photos

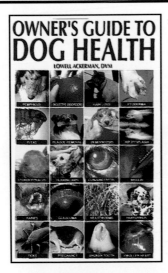

TS-249
Owner's Guide to Dog Health
Dr. Lowell Ackerman, DVM
224 pages, over 190 full-color photos

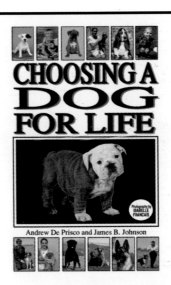

TS-257
Choosing a Dog for Life
Andrew DePrisco and James B. Johnson
384 pages, over 800 full-color photos

INDEX